DISCOVERING THE ORIGIN OF
HUMAN LIFE

by Todd Kortemeier

www.12StoryLibrary.com

12-Story Library is an imprint of Peterson Publishing Company and Press Room Editions.

Produced for 12-Story Library by Red Line Editorial

Photographs ©: Frank Franklin II/AP Images, cover, 1; John Gould, 5; Jose Angel Astor Rocha/ Shutterstock Images, 6; Paul Nicklen/National Geographic Creative/Corbis, 7; José-Manuel Benito Álvarez, 8; flowcomm CC2.0, 9, 28; Comaniciu Dan/Shutterstock Images, 10; Mopic/ Shutterstock Images, 11; vitstudio/Shutterstock Images, 12; Yatra/Shutterstock Images, 13; AuntSpray/Shutterstock Images, 14; Eduardo Estellez/Shutterstock Images, 15; Bryn Pinzgauer CC2.0, 16, 29; Rosie Young/Shutterstock Images, 17; Petter Bøckman, 19; Courtesy NASA/JPL-Caltech, 20; Public Domain, 21; Monkey Business Images/Shutterstock Images, 22; R. Rodenhausen/Shutterstock Images, 23; Pressmaster/Shutterstock Images, 24; Jaco Becker/Shutterstock Images, 25; Alzbeta/Shutterstock Images, 26; Lee Roger Berger research team, 27

Content Consultant: Scott A. Williams, Ph.D., Assistant Professor, Department of Anthropology, New York University

Library of Congress Cataloging-in-Publication Data

Cataloging-in-publication information is on file with the Library of Congress.
978-1-63235-376-4 (hardcover)
978-1-63235-393-1 (paperback)
978-1-62143-517-4 (hosted ebook)

Printed in the United States of America
Mankato, MN
May, 2016

Mississippi Mills
Public Library

12 STORY LIBRARY

Access free, up-to-date content on this topic plus a full digital version of this book. Scan the QR code on page 31 or use your school's login at 12StoryLibrary.com.

Table of Contents

Charles Darwin Publishes the Theory of Evolution

Charles Darwin was a naturalist. He studied plants, animals, and their environments. He lived during the 1800s in the United Kingdom. He came from a family of scientists. Both his father and grandfather were doctors. They were also interested in studying the world around them. Darwin developed the same interests.

As a boy, Darwin noticed the differences among bugs he found. He collected samples. He learned how to observe species. A species is a group of living things that all share the same features.

Darwin earned a spot as a scientist on a ship at the age of 22. The ship set sail in 1831. It was a nearly five-year voyage aboard the HMS *Beagle*. He went all around the world. He observed the plants and animals he found on the voyage. He saw animals few people had seen.

In the Galápagos Islands of South America, he made some of his most important findings. He noted many differences within a species of bird. Darwin believed the differences

DARWIN'S TORTOISES

While Darwin was in the Galápagos Islands, one of the species he observed was the Galápagos tortoise. These huge creatures weigh almost 500 pounds (230 kg) and live very long lives. They regularly live for more than 100 years. The oldest on record lived to be 152. That means tortoises born when Darwin visited in 1835 likely outlived him by more than 50 years.

1. Geospiza magnirostris. 2. Geospiza fortis.
3. Geospiza parvula. 4. Certhidea olivacea.

40,000

Approximate distance, in miles (64,400 km), of Darwin's voyage aboard the *Beagle*.

- Charles Darwin was a scientist who studied plants and animals.
- As a boy, he collected bugs and observed the differences among them.
- He sailed to countries around the world and observed thousands of animals.
- He believed species change over time in order to better survive.
- This process was called natural selection, and today it is well accepted by scientists.

Darwin noticed Galápagos finches from the same species had differently shaped beaks.

between birds showed that species evolve, or change, over time.

Darwin proposed that some changes help a species survive. Animals with these changes live long enough to mate. They pass the changes on to the next generation. Animals with changes that do not help them survive die more quickly. Their traits do not get passed on. Darwin called this process natural selection.

Darwin published his findings in a book called *On the Origin of Species*. His ideas did not fit with those of scientists at the time. Most people believed every living species was created and did not change. But slowly, Darwin's ideas became accepted. Today, Darwin is credited with developing the theory of evolution by natural selection. This is accepted by most scientists as the way all life, including humans, developed on Earth.

Fossils Provide the First Clues

Charles Darwin did not write about humans as part of his theory of evolution. There were few fossils to suggest that humans had changed with time. The first human fossil was not discovered until 1856. That's three years before *On the Origin of Species* was published.

Miners in Germany found the top part of a skull. But scientists at the time did not understand it. It looked like a human skull. But it was thicker, especially above where the eyes would have been.

THE OLDEST, MOST COMPLETE HUMAN

Any kind of human fossil is a rare find. It is even rarer to find a whole human skeleton. In 2014, scientists found the oldest and most complete humanlike skeleton ever. It was found in an underwater cave in Mexico. The skeleton is believed to be from a teenage girl approximately 4 feet 10 inches (1.5 m) tall. The fossil is estimated to be 12,000 to 13,000 years old.

Early humanlike skulls are much different from human skulls today.

Scientists thought it was a recent human who had been disfigured in some way. They did not notice the skull was found among long-extinct species of animals. That would have been a clue it was an ancient ancestor of humans.

The only way to trace human development was to study more fossils. But it took a long time for scientists to find more. In the late 1880s, a man named Eugène Dubois discovered remains of a creature that looked like an ape. But it stood more upright than an ape does. This feature was evidence the bones were remains of an early human ancestor.

At first, scientists did not believe Dubois's theory. But soon, more fossils were discovered. They proved the remains were a human ancestor. Today, this ancestor is known as *Homo erectus*.

6 million

Approximate age, in years, of the oldest humanlike fossil discovered.

- Darwin's theory was originally hard to apply to humans because few human fossils had been found.
- The first human fossil was found in 1856.
- Some scientists did not believe the fossil was evidence of ancient humans.
- Eugène Dubois discovered the first official known human ancestor in the late 1880s.

Africa Is the "Cradle of Humankind"

Darwin wrote in 1871 that he believed humans evolved in Africa. His reasoning was simple. Many species of apes lived in Africa. Apes are the closest relatives to humans. But for many years, most humanlike fossils were found in Europe and Asia. It wasn't until years later that evidence was found to support Darwin's theory.

In 1924, a shipment of rocks arrived at the home of Raymond Dart. Dart was a leading paleontologist. He was getting ready for a wedding when the two boxes arrived. He was dressed in nice clothing. But he

7 million

Estimated number of years ago that humans split from apes in evolution.

- In 1871, Darwin proposed Africa as the site of human evolution.
- Raymond Dart discovered the Taung Child in South Africa in 1924. Similar fossils were found soon after.
- Evidence that the creatures walked upright indicates they were human ancestors.
- Africa is called the "Cradle of Humankind" because of how many fossils come from there.

Skull of the Taung Child

Model of *Australopithecus africanus*, the species of the Taung Child

THINK ABOUT IT

If humans began in Africa, how do you think they got all around the world? For example, North America is across the ocean from Africa. What did the geography of Earth look like so that migration was possible?

could not wait to look through the rocks. What he found was stunning. Attached to one of the rocks was evidence of the brain cavity of a skull. Its shape and size led him to believe it was human. Further digs at the same site in South Africa revealed more of the skull. It appeared to be from a small child who had lived nearly 3 million years ago. Today, this ancestor is known as the Taung Child.

Other scientists at the time dismissed Dart's specimen as an ape. But by the 1930s, more evidence of the same species was found in South Africa. The fossils showed these creatures walked

upright. That is a key feature in humans, not apes. In the following decades, more humanlike fossils were found in eastern Africa.

Today, Africa is known as the "Cradle of Humankind." Most of the evidence we have for early human life has come from this continent. And scientists are not done. Fossil hunters have explored only approximately three percent of Africa.

Scientists Have Ways of Dating Objects

To understand the origin of human life, we need to know the timeline. What species came first? Who descended from whom? To answer these questions, scientists must put dates on fossils. There are a number of ways they do this.

One method is called carbon dating. Carbon 14 is something all living things absorb. They stop taking it in when they die. It then starts to to fade away

with time. Scientists can tell how old an object is based on how much carbon 14 is left in it. But all traces of carbon 14 are gone after 60,000 years. So scientists must use a different method for objects older than that.

Potassium-argon dating can be used to date much older fossils. Newly formed volcanic rock does not contain argon gas. But over time, a certain type of potassium in the rock turns into argon. Scientists know

Scientists can measure how much carbon 14 is in a fossil to find its age.

3.3 million

Age, in years, of the oldest human-made tools ever found.

- Scientists must determine the ages of fossils to create a timeline.
- One method of determining age is carbon dating, which is based on the amount of carbon 14 in a fossil.
- Potassium-argon dating is able to date volcanic rock that is billions of years old.
- Dates of changes in Earth's magnetic field are known and can be used to date rocks.

Earth's magnetic field has reversed in the past. The reversal is recorded in rock patterns.

how long this change takes. They can measure how much argon is in a rock. This tells them how old the rock is. Layers of rock above and below a fossil show the fossil's age. Potassium-argon dating can date rocks that are billions of years old.

Scientists also use Earth's magnetic field to find out the age of fossils. The direction of this field has changed many times. Scientists know the dates of these changes. A rock's age can be determined based on the magnetic pattern of the rock. The layer in which a fossil is found indicates the era that animal lived and died in.

DNA Shows How Close Humans Are to Ancestors

DNA is the genetic code for every living thing. Everyone's DNA is unique. It tells the body how to develop. DNA helps determine what color your hair is and how tall you will be. DNA is an important part of studying evolution. By comparing DNA, we can see how similar two species are. This helps scientists see whether one evolved from another.

Individual humans are very closely related. Any human's DNA is only approximately 0.1 percent different from another. But humans and apes are closely related, too. Human DNA is approximately 1.2 percent different from chimpanzees and bonobos. A gorilla's genes are 1.6 percent different from a human's.

Humans, gorillas, bonobos, and chimpanzees are part of a family called hominids. Scientists classify humans this way based on fossil and DNA evidence.

Nearly all living cells contain DNA.

The chimpanzee is one of the human's closest DNA relatives.

Humans have small differences in DNA that help make each person unique. But some parts of human DNA stay the same through many generations. These sections of DNA change only occasionally through random mutations. Scientists call these changes *markers*.

As people migrate and settle in new places, they gain certain markers. Studying markers can help identify the paths humans took to settle around the world. For example, there is a marker almost all people on Earth have. The people who do not have it are almost all from Africa. That means a small group of people probably came out of Africa and started the rest of the world's population.

20

Estimated number of people in the first group that settled in North America and began its population.

- DNA is the unique genetic code for every living thing.
- Human DNA is very similar to that of apes.
- That similarity supports the idea that humans evolved in Africa.
- Scientists use DNA markers to trace the path of human migration.

Climate Change Shapes Human Evolution

People sometimes call the process of natural selection "the survival of the fittest." But the fastest and strongest are not always the ones that survive. The ones with the best adaptations for their environment survive. One big factor in how a species adapts is climate.

Changes in Earth's climate have affected how humans have changed over time. One example is

diet. Some periods were cold, such as the Ice Age. Humans had to move to find food during this time. Other periods were hot. Grasslands may have dried up. Human ancestors who relied on these grasses had to adapt. Animals they hunted ate grass. The humans had to find other ways of getting food. This need may have led early humans to create tools in order to hunt.

Species, including the woolly mammoth, died off because they could not adapt to changes in climate.

11,700

Approximate number of years since the most recent Ice Age, in which ice covered most of North America.

- Natural selection is a key part of the theory of evolution.
- Climate change has caused many human adaptations.
- In hotter, drier times, humans had to adapt to different food sources.
- Early adaptations are still seen in modern humans' ability to think and problem-solve.

These changes were necessary to survive. Humans needed to use intelligence to solve the problem. Using their brains in this way shaped many of the unique aspects of modern humans.

There is evidence humans created hand axes for cutting more than 1.5 million years ago.

Changing climate may have even affected the human brain. Brain size increased the most during the greatest period of climate change. In hotter periods on Earth, lakes dried up. Some early humans depended on these lakes. Without them, humans had to think of other ways to get food.

"Hobbits" Lived in Asia

Humans have looked different during the millions of years they have existed. We would barely recognize some of them as human. Perhaps none were more different than early humans who lived in Indonesia. Between Asia and Australia lies the island Flores. It was home to tiny humans thousands of years ago.

Scientists discovered bones from small skeletons in Flores in 2004. They nicknamed them "hobbits," after the tiny characters in J. R. R. Tolkien's *Lord of the Rings* books. The first one they found

The "hobbit" fossils were found in a cave in Indonesia.

1/3
Approximate size of a "hobbit's" brain relative to modern humans.

- Humans have looked different throughout evolution.
- Fossils found in Indonesia in 2004 are from the smallest humans ever found.
- The "hobbits" lived at approximately the same time as some modern humans.
- Despite their small brains, "hobbits" had many of the same skills as modern humans.

Scientists believe that because Flores was remote, food may have been hard to find.

THINK ABOUT IT

People from some countries are shorter on average than people from other countries. Why do you think humans evolved to be different heights? What are some of the advantages? What are some other adaptations humans have undergone because of where they live?

was female. She was 3 feet 4 inches (1.0 m) tall. She weighed approximately 55 pounds (25 kg). But she was not a child. Scientists estimated she was 30 years old when she died.

What is so significant about these creatures is when they lived. They existed as recently as 50,000 years ago. That means modern humans were around at the same time. It was a major discovery that vastly different humans lived at the same time. Humans were more diverse than previously thought.

The "hobbits" were also advanced. They made fire and used tools. Despite having brains much smaller than modern humans' brains, they

had many of the same skills. One mystery is why these people were so small. A theory for their size is that their island was so remote. Food sources were harder to find. So they may have evolved to need fewer resources.

This discovery has prompted more exploration of Southeast Asia. There could be even more fossils of extreme humans out there.

17

The Missing Link Does Not Exist

Evolution is a long process in which species change and develop. For a long time, people did not know much about how humans evolved. No human fossils had been discovered. Some people believed we would find evidence humans developed from other species, such as chimpanzees. They thought we would find fossils that showed the change. People called these fossils *missing links*.

But evolution is not a ladder or chain. Species do not evolve in one long line. Evolution is more like a tree. It has many branches. Species that branch off of the tree continue to change. The species we see today, including chimpanzees, have not always looked like they do now. They have gone through their own evolutions.

Today, we have many human fossils that show how humans changed. These fossils are called transitional fossils. But the record is not complete. It would be almost impossible to find a complete record to span 1 billion years. But the fossils we have show a helpful picture of how humans evolved.

There were two huge changes in humans over the course of

6,000
Approximate number of early human individuals for which fossils have been found.

- A missing link is a species that links two other species in evolution.
- The missing-link theory is not in line with evolution.
- Transitional fossils show how species have evolved.
- Transitional fossils provide strong evidence for evolution.

BIGFOOT

Bigfoot is thought to be a big and hairy creature that looks like an ape. People today have claimed to spot it. But little evidence exists. Because bigfoot is said to walk upright, some believe it is the missing link between nonhuman apes and humans. Scientists could study bones and DNA to figure out how bigfoot is related to humans. But no bigfoot remains have been found.

their evolution. One was brain size. Early human brains did not approach the size of a modern human's until 500,000 years ago. Another change was walking upright. Humans have been walking upright for more than 4 million years. But they gradually lost grasping feet. And they stood up straighter. Transitional fossils give strong evidence for how humans evolved.

19

Homo sapiens Are Basically Brand-New

Every living thing on Earth has a scientific name. Humans are called *Homo sapiens.* This species showed up approximately 200,000 years ago. That's pretty old. But Earth is more than 4.5 billion years old. In Earth's history, humans have not been around very long.

Even the earliest believed human ancestor is not that old. Humanlike creatures did not start to emerge until approximately 2.5 million years ago. But even early *Homo sapiens* had a lot of differences from modern humans. The species has continued to evolve.

Modern humans are far different from what they were 10,000 years ago. For most of human history, humans have had to find their own food. They gradually started to use tools to help with this process. Within the last 12,000 years, most

Until approximately 12,000 years ago, humans were hunters and gatherers.

Humans have been farming for thousands of years.

humans have begun producing their own food. With access to plenty of food, humans set up cities. The population quickly grew. These factors have helped humans become the planet's dominant species. This is despite being a relatively young species.

Evidence shows human evolution is still going on. Within only the last 50 years, human diets have changed in big ways. One way is how humans digest milk. Most nonhuman mammals stop digesting milk after they no longer receive it from their mothers. Many humans have evolved to consume milk and other dairy products into their adult years. In the future, other changes may await.

760 million

Age, in years, of a sea sponge species that is believed to be the oldest species on Earth.

- Modern humans belong to the species *Homo sapiens*.
- *Homo sapiens* are approximately 200,000 years old.
- Humans have evolved to produce food and control their environments.
- Human evolution continues today.

Humans Are Still Evolving, but Differently

It might seem as if humans have stopped evolving. People have looked the same for a long time. And Darwin's theory of evolution by natural selection doesn't seem to apply either. With the advancements in medical care, survival is not a problem for most people. Humans live longer than ever. But this is a fairly recent trend. In the 1860s, only 67 percent of babies survived into adulthood. By the 1940s, it was 94 percent.

Medical care has improved the likelihood of babies reaching adulthood.

73

Average height of a man, in inches (1.9 m), of the tallest nation on Earth, the Netherlands.

- More humans are surviving into adulthood now than in the past.
- Natural selection is still at play in human genes.
- Evidence shows changes in genes, which is proof of more evolution.
- Humans have become resistant to disease and in some cases have been getting taller.

So how are humans still evolving? It's in our genes. Genes make up DNA, a human's unique code. Natural selection is still at work on that small level. In comparing modern human genes to other apes' genes, they show different kinds of changes. This shows that humans are continuing to evolve away from ape ancestors.

Humans are now stronger against diseases. Outbreaks used to kill millions of people. Descendants of people who survived have much stronger immune systems than their ancestors. People in the future will have even more immunities.

There have been more visible changes too. People are getting taller. Average height varies by country. But in the United Kingdom,

THE APPENDIX

Humans and other apes have an organ called the appendix. Its function in the body has been a mystery for a long time. Darwin thought it had no purpose. Scientists now think the appendix has evolved more than 30 times. That implies that it has grown and changed to suit the needs of humans. And other mammals have similar organs. The appendix may help protect helpful bacteria in the body.

the average height of young men has gone up four inches (10.2 cm) since 1900. One possible reason is that taller people are more successful on average. The evolutionary forces that got humans to this point are still in progress.

Human Teeth May Have Shrunk from Tool Use

Teeth are a common human fossil to find. They are harder than bone and last for a long time. So scientists do a lot of research with the teeth of humans and other apes.

One mystery of the evolution of teeth is why they've gotten smaller

with time. This can be seen with wisdom teeth. In modern humans, these teeth are small. Sometimes they never even develop. But in human ancestors, these teeth were two to four times larger.

One theory for smaller teeth is that the modern human diet changed to

Human teeth have shrunk over time.

1

Percentage decrease in human tooth size every 1,000 years for the past 10,000 years.

- Teeth are commonly found fossils because they are the hardest part of the human body.
- Scientists have observed that human teeth get smaller with time.
- Scientists now believe human teeth became smaller as humans started using tools.
- Knowing that tooth size decreases over time can help date fossils.

make wisdom teeth unnecessary. But some scientists now think small teeth could be due to humans using tools. Tools made it easier to cook. And diets changed. So humans did not need such big teeth to chew and grind up primitive food.

Knowing this, scientists can compare the teeth of human ancestors from different eras. Shrinking teeth can help scientists know where different species came in human evolution. In

hard-to-date fossils, a discovery like this could provide the missing clues.

Species' teeth give clues about what they eat.

THINK ABOUT IT

In the animal kingdom, teeth come in all shapes and sizes. What factors do you think influence what kind of teeth an animal has? Why do humans have teeth with different shapes?

Homo naledi Challenges Thoughts on Early Humans

Fossil evidence has helped scientists put together a timeline of human origins. But that can always change when a new fossil is found. In 2015, a discovery did just that. A new species was discovered in a cave in South Africa. More than 1,500 fossil remains were found. It was the largest single human fossil discovery in Africa. Called *Homo naledi*, the species challenges a lot of what scientists thought they knew.

It is believed that the remains were found in a cave because they were buried there. But burial of the dead is a much more recent human behavior. And *Homo naledi* likely needed fire to be able to see in the caves. But their skulls showed they had very small brains. This behavior seemed too difficult for them to handle.

Before finding *Homo naledi*, it was thought that burial was a more recent practice.

7

Width, in inches (18 cm), of the narrowest part of the cave scientists had to get through to find *Homo naledi*.

- Scientists discovered a new species of early human in 2015.
- *Homo naledi* was discovered in a cave in South Africa.
- With more than 1,500 fossils, it was the largest find in Africa.
- The find indicates human ancestors may have buried their dead earlier than previously thought.

But this discovery shows that there is still much to learn about early humans.

Bones from many individuals were found in the South African cave. Scientists put them together to form a skeleton.

It was difficult to date the fossils. There was not much other evidence to help. But based on what the skeletons looked like, and the small brain size, they had to be older than 100,000 years. It will take much more research to find exactly where *Homo naledi* fits in human history.

Fact Sheet

- Modern humans are the last remaining species of the family Hominidae. Approximately 70,000 years ago, there were four human species on Earth. More than 12 human species have been discovered in Earth's history. More than 6,000 fossils of those species have been found.

- It's often said humans came from monkeys. Although monkeys are a close relative, and they share a common ancestor, humans are not descended from any living primate. The common ancestor of humans and apes last lived approximately 7 million years ago.

- Humans looked the same until approximately 60,000 years ago. That's when people started to develop different skin colors and facial features.

- Bone problems affect modern humans more than they affected our ancestors. Walking upright puts a lot of stress on two legs. Bones of early humans were also thicker and stronger than they are today.

Humans are distinguished by their large brains. The human brain grew in size most rapidly during periods of climate change. Humans had to learn to think critically to find new sources of food. Humans also invented tools to make tasks easier. For a long time, it was thought only humans used tools. But some other species do, too.

Glossary

ancestor
In humans, a person from whom others are descended.

ape
A family of primates that includes humans.

extinct
When all individuals of a species die.

fossil
Evidence of a once-living thing.

gene
A basic unit of life that influences one's traits.

mammal
Animals that share several characteristics including hair, a spine, and giving birth to live babies.

miner
A person who works in a mine digging for coal or other minerals.

mutations
Permanent changes in hereditary materials.

organ
A part of the body that performs a task for that body.

skull
The bones that collectively make up the head.

species
A group of living things that are similar and can produce young.

For More Information

Books

Hustad, Douglas. *Charles Darwin Develops the Theory of Evolution.* Minneapolis, MN: Abdo Publishing, 2016.

Solway, Andrew. *Why Is There Life on Earth?* Chicago: Raintree, 2015.

Tattersall, Ian. *The Great Human Journey: Around the World in 22 Million Years.* Piermont, NH: Bunker Hill, 2013.

Visit 12StoryLibrary.com

Scan the code or use your school's login at **12StoryLibrary.com** for recent updates about this topic and a full digital version of this book. Enjoy free access to:

- Digital ebook
- Breaking news updates
- Live content feeds
- Videos, interactive maps, and graphics
- Additional web resources

Note to educators: Visit 12StoryLibrary.com/register to sign up for free premium website access. Enjoy live content plus a full digital version of every 12-Story Library book you own for every student at your school.

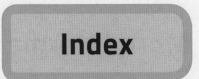

Index

About the Author

Todd Kortemeier is a writer from Minneapolis, Minnesota. He is a graduate of the University of Minnesota's School of Journalism & Mass Communication. He has authored many books for young people.

READ MORE FROM 12-STORY LIBRARY

Every 12-Story Library book is available in many formats. For more information, visit 12StoryLibrary.com.